SECRETS

SECRETS

BY PAUL TOURNIER

Translated by Joe Embry

JOHN KNOX PRESS
Richmond, Virginia

Adapted from a lecture given at Athens in the Hall of the
Archeology Society, May 12, 1963.

Original French edition entitled *Le Secret* published by
Éditions Labor et Fides, Geneva, 1963.

International Standard Book Number: 0-8042-2165-X
Library of Congress Catalog Card Number: 65-13442
© M. E. Bratcher 1965
Printed in the United States of America

Fourth printing 1970

CONTENTS

I THE NEED OF SECRECY, OR THE FIRST STAGE IN THE FORMATION OF THE INDIVIDUAL

A little girl is coming home from school. Her name is Frances. Until now her mother had always taken her and gone to get her. It wasn't very far: a street running uphill. Frances and her mother would sometimes take the sidewalk on the left, which ran by stores with their beautiful display windows, sometimes the walk on the other side where there were no stores.

But now her mother considers her big enough to let her go alone. For every child, the day when he's allowed to go to school alone denotes an important promotion. Frances was quite proud and is now radiantly returning home; she hugs her mother's neck. The latter is even more emotional and quizzes her sharply: "Did it go all right? Did you walk by yourself? Were you with some friends? Did you take the store side of the street or the other one?"

Under this flood of questions, Frances feels completely ill at ease. "I took the store side," she says. And yet, she had indeed taken the other side. She is quite astonished, herself, a little confused, having answered thus. Is it a lie? After all, what importance does it make whether she took the sidewalk on one side rather than the other? And why did this false answer come out of her mouth before she had even thought?

But also why then did her mother ask her that question? Why does she want to know which sidewalk she took? Basically, probably, her mother doesn't consider it important. She only needed to talk, to ask questions, lots of questions, as a release for her emotion. The result was this flood of questions which Frances resented because it was prying. If her mother considers her big enough to go to school by herself now, she should no longer demand that Frances tell her everything she has done.

No, Frances has not told a lie. She is a very good and very candid little girl, who came straight home from school without having a good time on the way. She feels in a perplexed way that she has answered that way in order to have a secret. She would not be able to hide anything important from her mother. But she is beginning to need to no longer tell her everything, now that she can go to school by herself. She needs to have a secret, at least a tiny little secret. That is exactly what is important; and that is what her mother has not understood; she has indiscreetly plied her with questions in order to learn everything.

Yes, until birth, the child is only a part of his mother. It doesn't matter if the umbilical cord is cut; for a long time he will remain absolutely tied to her. He is not yet an individual; he is still only his mother's baby, totally dependent on her. When he talks, he will need to tell her everything, even his secrets, even that which he will tell no one else. My father expressed it in one of his poems for children:[1]

> On his mama's knees
> Little Peter is seated, quiet, a long moment,
> Then, questioning her: sweet mother,
> A secret, say, what is it?
> —It's something that you know,
> But you must keep it quiet from the rest of the world.

[1] Louis Tournier, *Les Enfantines* (Geneva: Jeheber).

—Even from your mama?—No, a child must never
Have any secret from his mother.—Oh, well!
In that case, I see what must be done:
I'm going to tell you mine.
And leaning toward her, with mystery:
Mama, mama, I love you very much . . .
The mother looks at him then tenderly,
Then kissing him: "Your secret, it's mine.
From now on, also, I shall keep it,
My darling, I shall say nothing about it . . ."

The years pass. The child grows; he goes to school; he goes to
school by himself. He will have to free himself little by little from
his mother, from his parents, in order to become an individual. And
his secrets are going to be the indispensable instruments of this
emancipation. It is to the extent that he has secrets from his parents
that he gains an awareness of self; it is to the extent that he becomes
free to keep his secrets from them that he gets an awareness of being
distinct from them, of having his own individuality, of being a person.

Our little Frances was obeying this law of life without knowing it,
without having reasoned it out, spontaneously, and even astonished at
her own reaction. She was beginning to need a secret; she was beginning to need to become an individual and no longer only her
mother's daughter. Until then her mother could ask her any question
whatsoever without her seeing anything in it but what her mother
put into it: her tender concern for her daughter. And suddenly
Frances resents a question as if it were prying.

And she resists this intrusion of her mother into her private life which is beginning; she resists the instinctive need which she felt until then, to tell everything to her mother. She will escape henceforth from the all-powerful hold of her mother over her. So, to have secrets, to know how to keep them to one's self, to give them up only willingly, constitutes the first action in the formation of the individual.

In his fine book *The Discovery of Self*,[2] Mr. Georges Gusdorf quotes a significant page from the memoirs of Edmond Gosse, who "one day, in his childhood, when it was a question of an incident of little importance, an unpunished lie, discovered that his absolute confidence in the almighty power of his father did not correspond to reality." "Belief in the omniscience and infallibility of my father," wrote Gosse, "was now dead and buried. There was a secret in this world, and this secret belonged to me and to someone who lived in my body. And there were two of us, and we could talk with each other. It was under this form of dualism that the sense of my individuality appeared to me suddenly, at that very moment, and it was equally certain that it was a great consolation to find in myself someone who could understand me."

Yes, the child—and the adult too, of course—talks to himself constantly; he tells himself all his secrets; he knows all his own secrets. And that is what gives him a feeling of identity with himself and with himself alone. I imagine that Edmond Gosse had already had many secrets before the memorable day of which he speaks here. But he doubtlessly had not yet clearly had an awareness of it. Almost all children's games have already a flavor of secrecy. When he turns a chair upside down and pretends that it is a ship, it is truly for him

[2] Georges Gusdorf, *La découverte de soi* (Paris: Presses Universitaires de France, 1948).

a ship. And that corner of the room toward which he is headed is Marseilles, or New York, where he is going to disembark.

The pleasure of the game consists in part in that, for everyone else, this chair is only a chair, and that corner is only a corner of the room, while for him this chair is a ship and that corner a port. It is his secret. However, it is possible to not yet have completely an awareness of individuality: if this child is at the age when Edmond Gosse still believed "in the omniscience and the infallibility of his father," he can grant his father, in a more or less confused way, the knowledge of his secret; and if his father calls this chair: chair, and not ship, it is doubtlessly out of consideration for him that he does not divulge the secret. And this feeling that his father knows all his secrets is still for him, at this age, pleasing.

But what an upheaval when the child perceives that he knows something that certainly no one but he knows, not even his father, nor his mother! Therefore, they don't know everything. The child experiences a quite new feeling of power, for he has an awareness of possessing something in his own right, his very own. Until then, everything he owned, he got from his parents or at least with their consent. He acquires a truly personal possession only by receiving or getting something without their knowledge.

Or yet by undertaking something secretly: there are some games which are really work: research in natural history; construction of a real boat, or of a very complicated electrical or mechanical device; the pursuit of an invention which the child hopes will make him famous. Then he goes about his business very secretly. It is not easy to find a place safe from prying looks or from the good housekeeper who throws in the garbage can everything which she claims is of no use.

Fortunately there is an attic, or an obliging pal who has the use of a hut at the back of his yard! Often secrecy depends on the fear the child has that grown-ups will make fun of him and his undertakings, or that they will say to him: "You are always beginning things, but you never finish them." On reaching a certain age every child needs secrecy, and even more so as he grows up. Consider those thousand little odd and insignificant objects that he collects as still a very small child, that he clings to lovingly, with which he peoples his private world. Hands off! They are his little secrets, what is truly his own, much more so than the beautiful toys he can take out of the closet only with the permission of his parents.

A certain feeling of power is always attached to the keeping of a secret. Doubtlessly the extreme fascination that secrets hold over every child is due to that reason. When one of his pals insinuates: "I know something you don't, but I won't tell you," he won't stop trying to get the secret out of him. He will use every means, intimidation, pleading, or trickery, first one, then the other, or will try to buy the revelation of the secret by offering one of his toys to his pal. This latter is proud of himself if he is able to resist all these attempts. He will still enjoy his superiority, even when he tells his secret. In case of need he may invent one, for he may have boasted rashly of one he didn't have. Every child is proud of having a secret.

Fascination with secrecy! Consider the mysterious preparations for Christmas, how they excite children and increase the prestige of the celebration! The children secretly make up a gift for papa and a gift for mama and take great pains that their parents won't guess or discover the surprise in advance. And the decoration of the tree is a secret between papa and the boy, who has been allowed to come help.

But afterward, the door of the room is locked, and papa puts the key in his pocket: mama or little sister must not see the tree before the celebration. Even at the last moment, it is very secretly that father and son sneak in by the tree to light the candles, and it is not until then that they solemnly open the door. Children know that parents also have their secrets, presents which they have prepared and carefully wrapped the night before, when the children were in bed.

All of that exercises a magical attraction which depends on secrets, and on that impatience to discover them which every secret arouses in every human soul. They all know that there will be a Christmas celebration, that there will be a lighted tree, that there will be presents. But it is necessary, with a common accord, by many precautions, to arouse mystery, to increase the charm. Each child shows to his brothers and sisters the gifts which he secretly prepares for his parents: an emotional bond is established between those who know the same secret which they agree to hide from everyone else.

The great relish children have for secret languages is derived from that. It permits them, even at the family table, to exchange messages whose meaning escapes the adults. And it is a revenge on adults, on the tyrannical power they exercise. Don't they claim that nothing escapes them, that a little birdie tells them everything? And don't they speak among themselves a foreign language when they don't want children to understand what they say?

But the child confers on all kinds of things a secret meaning to create for himself a little world all his own, safe from prying. When a locomotive whistle blasts forth nearby, the great green dragon has broken through the screen of fire to go devour the prey that a good fairy, fortunately, snatches from him. And isn't the fairy's combat

with the dragon more poetic and more exciting than the locomotive which is going through a grade crossing?

Yes, secrets, you can invent an infinite number of them, and that also is a revenge that the child takes on his real life so strictly hemmed in by the prudence of his parents and by moral principles, both of which are opposed to any fantasy which is too exaggerated or dangerous. Every child narrates marvelous stories to himself, and the happiest child is the one who never runs short of imagination. But the wonderful flavor of these tales depends precisely on their secrecy. Because the child is the only one to know them, whereas his real life is well known by everyone.

However, the child quickly realizes that adults also have their secrets and that there are some especially charged with emotion; these secrets fascinate him in the highest degree. These are things that adults never talk about in front of him and to which some friend, someone older, or some person outside the family, makes mysterious allusions. If he questions his parents, they answer him sharply: "That will be explained to you when you are older." All that does is to excite even more so his curiosity. Moreover he understands that he must manage for himself to pierce the mystery.

How do children come into the world? His father indeed told him one day in a solemn and embarrassed fashion that they developed in their mother's abdomen "quite near the heart." But this summary answer raises in his mind many more questions than it solves. What sets off this development of the child? How does the birth take place? And then, what does this word "adultery" or "homosexual" mean, which he has overheard by chance? Or this word "sex-appeal" which he saw on the cover of a magazine stuck up at the corner newsstand?

On the sly he looks for explanations in his father's dictionary, and this secrecy, this fear of being caught, increases his excitement. But the definitions that he finds are quite obscure! Decidedly, adults' secrets are well protected. He furtively opens a novel that his mother always carefully puts back under other books, but he doesn't find the page which must be the most interesting, or rather he finds one which must be speaking of these things, but in a way so concealed that he realizes quite well that the real secret is still escaping him. He comes back to it however, he reads it again often, with excitement, but without yet piercing the mystery. He furtively goes out of his way to pass by a park where there is a statue of a naked woman.

And when this child reaches puberty, whether a boy or a girl, what happens to him raises a flood of questions and anxieties. At times, he thinks he's in the grip of some shameful illness. He becomes more and more embarrassed by everything related to sex, at the same time that he is obsessed with it. He sinks more and more into secrecy to hide his thoughts and his acts. What fantastic turmoil these secrets can arouse in his soul; what an insurmountable barrier they raise henceforth between him and his parents!

Of course, I can depict all that with only a few broad strokes. The experience is different for every child, infinitely varied, but always filled with difficulties. No one reaches maturity without secret anguishes, secret searches, and secret remorses, even those whose parents are mature and free enough themselves not to add the burden of their own uneasiness to that of their children. For parents have problems too, secret problems also, sexual problems, and still many other problems.

The child has a quick intuition for what is hidden from him. Why does papa require him to go to catechism class while papa never goes to church himself? There's a secret there. Why do his parents never want to see his uncle Louis, who is so nice? There's a secret there. Why did his parents have such a gloomy look that night they sent him to bed earlier then usual? There's a secret there. Lying in his bed, the child strains to hear the slightest noise; he tries to catch a word from the garbled sounds which reach him. He gets up; he goes on tiptoe to the hall. He ponders over it; he puts his imagination to work.

Yes, because they conceal many things from him, the child imagines many secrets. A misunderstood word, a gesture, a silence, any one of them is enough for him to create a drama, to construct a story. Surely, his father is having an affair, and that is why his parents are quarreling so often. Or, rather, he is convinced that they are not his real parents; he is a foundling who had been stolen by gypsies, who ran away, and who has been taken in. That must be it, the big secret they hide from him. He doesn't dare ask for fear of having confirmed what he dreads. Or, on the other hand, his true father is another man, very rich, very powerful, very intelligent, and very good, who once seduced his mother, and whom he will find someday, no matter what it costs.

There is a reciprocal bond between secrecy and emotion. Secrecy makes things valuable. On the other hand, many important things take on an air of secrecy because they are discussed only in a confidential tone. "While still quite small," a woman told me, "I realized that sex and religion were shut up in the same secret closet!" From time immemorial religions have included secrets known only to their initiates. Every church has rites whose meanings have the prestige of secrecy. Each symbol, each formula, has a secret meaning which confers on it its sacred character.

When anyone enters a church which is unfamiliar to him, he feels ill at ease because he does not know its secrets. He carefully watches how other people act and is afraid of committing a blunder. The liturgy remains incomprehensible to him if its secret meanings have not been explained to him. The Bible itself is so obscure. It seems to me that that is a misfortune for our Protestant churches to have tried to explain everything about religion. It is perhaps for that reason that we see among some of them a revival of glossolalia, the speaking in tongues, which played such a great role in the primitive church. This confused muttering, incomprehensible without interpretation, expresses the inexpressible. Religion needs secrecy.

That is true, not only of churches, moreover, but of the nation, of every organized society. In a beautiful page of his memoirs,[3] C. G. Jung sets forth this absolute necessity, for every social formation, no matter how primitive it may be, to have a certain "secret organization," whose "common secret constitutes the cement of his interior cohesion." If, outside of my native land, I want to be recognized by a compatriot, I don't need to exhibit my passport to prove to him that I am from Geneva. It is enough to recite the magical formula of our childhood games: "Empro, Giro, Carin, Caro, Dupuis, Simon, Carcaille, Briffon, Piron, Labordon, Tan, Te, Feuille, Meuille, Tan, Te, Clu."

[3] C. G. Jung, *Traumereien und Memoiren*.

II RESPECT FOR THE INDIVIDUAL

Fascination of secrecy! Secrecy acts no less on adults than on children. What is it that gives classical tragedy its powerful hold? The fact that the audience knows a secret which the principal character does not know. Oedipus does not know he's going to kill his father and marry his mother. We would like to shout it at him. Even the lowest form of vaudeville, with its mistaken identities, derives its effects from a well-arranged game of secrets that certain characters know and which are unknown to others.

And detective novels! If they succeed in distracting a business man from his serious concerns, it is because he can't drop the book before the secret of the enigma is revealed to him. Every reader of a detective story feels awaken within himself an eager detective spirit which is hunting for the secret. And adventure novels and books on the great secrets of history, *Atlantis,* or *The Iron Mask*! And also the books on the little secrets of intimate history.

There are also illustrated weeklies which reveal the secrets of the private lives of movie stars with photographs taken with a telescopic lens; and the lampooning weeklies which reveal the petty weaknesses of important political figures. And the magazines of secret confession and true love stories. And gossip, which broadcasts neighbors' and friends' secrets: "But of course, everyone knows about it, Mr. Z. went bankrupt once." "He looks like such a steady person, Mr. Y.! Oh, ho! he's cheating on his wife with his secretary; his wife is the only one who doesn't know, but she is so stupid." "That dress which Mrs. X. shows off with so much pride, I assure you she bought it in a bargain

basement." Whoever runs short on such gossip can always easily make some up. He can even say with tact: "I won't tell you what I heard about Mrs. W." There are secret recipes that fashionable restaurants call specialties of the house which the obliging owner whispers in your ear. There are beauty secrets. There are the secrets of hunters and fishermen, their innumerable little tricks of success, which have their charm, even if they don't work. There are the secular secrets of healers, and the black magic secrets of conjurers.

In ancient times, the most powerful and most venerated man was the magician who knew the secrets of omens. Today, it is the scientist who competes with him for prestige, but the scientist owes it to his knowledge of the secrets of nature, to his skill in stealing her secrets little by little. Thanks to him, the secrets of the moon or of Mars will soon be unveiled. For the few men whose adventurous lives impress us, how many more men are there who nourish grandiose but secret ambitions in their bosoms, that they will never fulfill but which will have been however among the greatest joys of their lives?

For some women who find happiness in a happy marriage, how many women are there who must be satisfied with secret loves which they nourish in their hearts in spite of the suffering which accompanies them? In addition, how many secret sufferings and secret heartaches are there, which provide hidden treasures, in spite of their pain, which are perhaps, because secret, better hidden from the vicissitudes of life than many shameless pleasures?

Yes, secrecy is like a strongbox where we can piously keep treasures: some remembrance of some beautiful past, quite finished; some photograph carefully wrapped up and locked away; some manuscript begun with enthusiasm and which never dared confront publication, and

which stays there, with its nostalgia, in the bottom of a drawer; some painting that the amateur artist has never been able to finish; some intimate diary with innumerable notebooks. If I can believe the secrets which have been revealed to me, the documents which have been intrusted to me as a very special favor, these clandestine works are much more frequent than you would believe, and often of great value.

I know indeed moreover how delicate this question is. A creative work is a very fragile thing while it is being produced. It needs secrecy. It can die away, lose its impetus and its conviction by being divulged prematurely. I indeed see it in the case of the books I write and which I do not dare read to my wife before the work is quite far along, and I am grateful to her for understanding that, for tactfully respecting my sensitiveness. A criticism, a comment, even praise, can disrupt the creative impetus. However, it is indeed necessary, sooner or later, to confront them, under penalty of remaining forever a prisoner of this secrecy so necessary at the beginning. Likewise, people in love justly take great precautions to keep their romance a secret at its beginning, when it is still fragile. That is precisely what parents want to know all about, and they can completely spoil everything by their prying. But there are also loves which remain secret forever, through lack of having dared to be shown openly in time.

Yes, a certain secrecy, to just the right extent, ought to enclose every precious thing, every precious experience, so that it can mature and bear fruit. This remark takes us back to our little Frances who was beginning to need a secret in relation to her mother in order to become herself. I imagine that if this mother had realized that her daughter had not told her the exact truth, she would have scolded her sharply. She would have perhaps treated her as a liar and would have told her that lying is the worst of faults, especially with regard to a mother to whom a child must tell everything.

Most parents are very irritated when they realize that their child is hiding something from them. They do not understand how necessary it is to the child in order for him to become an individual. It is somewhat in the hope of opening their eyes that I am writing this book. What they understand very well is that their child is beginning to escape from them. And their anger is a very natural revolt against this breaking away of their child. They would like to prolong this frank communion, so sweet, so marvelous, which bound to them their child without reserve during his early years.

There are some who close their eyes to this occurrence. A mother brings me her adolescent daughter. "My daughter is my best friend," she reveals to me immediately; "we tell each other absolutely everything." I ask the mother then to leave us alone and the daughter talks to me for an hour of all sorts of things that she never mentions to her mother. Moreover the latter fabricates as many illusions about herself. She has constructed this myth that her daughter is her best friend. She is very proud of it and has such a great need of keeping it up that she no longer realizes at all that in reality she tells her daughter only what she wishes to tell her. It would moreover be very unfortunate if she told too many of her secrets to her daughter as many other mothers do.

Some parents become transformed into detectives. They go into the street, hidden in some doorway, to watch for their child, to see with what friend he comes home from school and what he is doing on the way. But when the child grows older and is more on guard, this inquisition can develop dramatic proportions. A mother came to see me to explain the concern her son was causing her and whom she wanted to send to me. She had forbidden him to see again a certain girl whose demeanor and reputation displeased her. Now, she has proof that they are carrying on a secret correspondence, that they send each other love letters, that they meet, as the girl's letters give evidence. I ask: "How do you know all that?" —"Oh! I had another key made for my son's drawer and I go read the letters when he's at school. I should, shouldn't I? It's my duty to keep watch over my son!" She is stupefied that I am not in agreement, and I ask her: "How can you expect your son to be honest with you if you are not with him?"

Without going that far, many parents gently make it understood to their children that they must go on telling them everything, just as when they were quite small. "I saw my friend B.," a mother tells her daughter. "It seems that you met her daughter yesterday and you even went for a walk together, and you didn't tell me about it. Fortunately, your friend tells her mother everything!"

In the face of such claims, such pressures from parents, there are two reactions possible for the child: a strong reaction—he is going to become more and more remote from them, hide more and more things from them, even harmless ones; he's going to live his life completely without their knowledge or participation, to close himself completely away from them, scheme, avoid, perhaps hate.

His parents will reproach him for it and continue to do so in a more and more violent fashion, at times going as far as open conflict, without realizing at all that they themselves have been the creators of this misfortune. But, on the other hand, the child may have a weak reaction: he capitulates; he thinks he's obligated to tell his parents everything always, to see only the friends of whom they approve, to do only what they suggest. This child indeed risks becoming ill. In any case, he will stop in his development, he will keep childish characteristics, he will be hesitant and timid. His parents will grieve over him as much as over the rebels with no greater realization that they are responsible for the situation.

Several times I have had a mother come to my office with a forty- or fifty-year-old son. She would do the talking for him, set forth his case for him, and then be astonished when I told her: "But your son is old enough to explain his case by himself." Alas! in the absence of his mother, he would not succeed in explaining much by himself because he had lost all capacity to think for himself. You also sometimes see a daughter forty or fifty years old who does not dare get a letter without having her mother read it, nor spend a dime of what she earns herself without asking her mother's permission.

In the thesis that she recently submitted to the Faculty of Medicine of the University of Montpellier, Dr. Suzanne Miguel justly states: "To have something private and secret is a characteristic of the individual."[1] The parents who deprive their older children of their private life prevent them from becoming individuals. The right to secrecy is a fundamental prerogative of the individual.

Every human being needs secrecy in order to become himself and no longer only a member of his tribe. It is one of the misfortunes of the present day that the living space of every family is more and more restricted: political and military events drive people before them and pile up refugees; building has not caught up with the increase

[1] Dr. Suzanne Miguel, *Vers une médecine de la personne*, Thesis (Montpellier, 1963).

in population; the profit motive is responsible for making apartments even smaller. In these conditions no one any longer has space of his own; parents, brothers, and sisters, all live on top of each other, without a secret corner all their own. Every human being needs secrecy in order to collect his thoughts and for others to respect his secrecy. To respect the secrecy of whoever it may be, even your own child, is to respect his individuality. To intrude upon his private life, to violate his secrecy, is to violate his individuality.

Now, parents have been accustomed so long to asking their child any question whatsoever that they do not at all have the impression of violating his individuality by continuing to do so. A day comes however, and sometimes rather suddenly, when they must stop asking him questions which have been simple and harmless up to that point: "When did you come home last night? I did not hear you."—"What do you plan to do next Sunday?"—"Were there many people at your friend Peter's house last night? Were Andrew L. and his sister there too?"—"Weren't you cold this morning? You left without your coat." —"That little watercolor that I saw in your room is very pretty: who gave it to you?"—"Do you feel ready for that bookkeeping exam? Does it worry you?"—"You often get letters written in such a small hand? Is your friend Daniel the one who writes that way?"

These questions, and many others of like nature, were welcomed a short while ago, as very natural expressions of tender care. Suddenly the child resents them as so much prying. He doesn't answer them anymore; his reply is an imperceptible shrug which means: "That's none of your business!" And his mother is hurt: "Truly," she thinks, "this boy is becoming too sensitive; you can't ask him anything anymore. However, I have to know if I must get his ski suit ready for Sunday! Life is becoming impossible with him; he regards his home as a hotel: he comes late to meals, eats hurriedly without saying anything, and leaves immediately afterward. I feel sorry for his wife when he's married."

It's precisely when he gets married that these problems are increased. This mother sets her mind to doing everything possible to get along with her daughter-in-law. She welcomes her with fervor as if she were her own daughter. She questions her with a great deal of affection; she wants to know all about her childhood, her views, how she met John, if the bedside lamp she gave her really pleases her. She wants to help her make a success of her marriage. She knows her son better than this young woman. He has whims: "You know, he doesn't like eggplant." She opens her closets and gives her good advice, with a lot of tact: it would be better not to put her husband's shirts under the pile of linen because he will mess everything up when he takes one out.

Why does this young wife look glum so often? She isn't easy to get along with. She could be grateful for being surrounded by such loving care. She must be made to feel that she is a part of the family; we can't remain strangers to each other. This mother doesn't think she's prying: those things however are not secrets. That is why it so unfortunate that young married couples, not being able to find an apartment, begin their married life in their parents' home. They have no secrets. Their parents know everything they do, when they go out, when they come home, if they stay in bed on Sunday morning or if they go to church.

And then there are John's sisters, who have also welcomed their sister-in-law with enthusiasm. How wonderful to have a bigger family now: she will be a real sister to them. They have always been so close together in the family. There were no secrets between them and their brother. They certainly don't want his marriage to harm this model relationship. Their sister-in-law must feel completely at home when she comes to see them, and they, too, feel at home when they go to their brother's home. You don't have any secrets from those you love! They, too, open closets and look to see if their sister-in-law wears nightgowns or pajamas.

All that is, alas, very commonplace, but also tragic. For quite often it is precisely the most affectionate and best-meaning zeal of parents which spoils their relations with the young couple. If their son has not broken away from them, as we have seen, if he has made only a feeble reaction to their intervention, if he doesn't dare either to defend his wife from their prying, he thinks she is too sensitive, suspicious, at times unjust with respect to them, and it is the very unity of the couple which is then in danger. Everyone has made a valiant effort and no one understands why it's turning out badly. There is a misunderstanding, but the misunderstanding is about a point whose importance was disregarded: secrecy, the vital secrecy for the formation of the individual first, then, for the formation of the couple.

What grants secrecy its capital value is that individuality is at stake and every violation of secrecy is a violation of that individuality. It has been seen with totalitarian regimes. They rest essentially on contempt for the individual. You may remember, for example, the tragic case of Landsberg's conscience,[2] when, as a prisoner of the Gestapo, he argued with himself, contemplating suicide for fear that torture would snatch

[2] Landsberg, *Essai sur l'expérience de la mort,* followed by *Problème moral du suicide* (Paris: Le Seuil, 1951).

from him his secret: the list of the other members of his Resistance network. He had been able to keep his little ampule of cyanide. Did he have the right to use it because of his fear of betraying his fellow conspirators? He finally judged that his Christian faith would not permit him to kill himself and he took upon himself his terrible risk. He died at the Oranienburg concentration camp without having revealed his secret.

You think perhaps that such extreme cases have no relationship to the family stories about which I was speaking. I do not believe it. Respect for the individual is an absolute requirement. Either we have the sense of it and keep it scrupulously, or else we have started down the dangerous road of tyranny. There is no middle of the road, no halfway measures. A germ of totalitarianism lies dormant in all the police forces of the world, none of which have too many scruples to use rough treatment. Everyone senses that. Every man feels intuitively what is sacred in secrecy, the responsibility that keeping a secret implies—state secrets, military secrets, industrial secrets, medical, judiciary, and business professional secrets, confessional secrets. Every man has an awareness of the dishonor imposed on any attempt to get hold of another man's secret through force or trickery, and on any disclosure of a secret through selfish motives or cowardice. But a germ of totalitarianism also lies dormant inside all of us. If it is not developed, it is simply because we are not powerful enough to become potentates with impunity. Many people severely criticize the great ones of this world without realizing at all that they themselves tyrannize their families, their subordinates, those about them, to the extent of the authority they possess. It is very dangerous for a man to be powerful.

That is indeed what Emmanuel Mounier,[3] the philosopher of egoism, felt, when he conducted, just before dying, his great investigation on "Medicine, Fourth Power" in his magazine *Esprit*. Science and modern techniques confer on the doctor a fearful power over man; fearful for the patient, but also fearful for the doctor. Mounier especially had in mind brain surgery, psychoanalysis, and analysis with narcotics. To what extent do you have the right to use techniques capable of pulling out of a man his secrets? I myself have answered that I sometimes use narcotics in analysis, that the matter does not seem capable of being solved by a general ruling, but depends essentially on the spirit which animates the doctor, on his profound respect for the human individual, on the free and sincere consent of the patient.

There, too, there is no middle of the road, no halfway measures. All medicine, no matter what technique, constitutes a power exercised on man. It is a question of knowing if we exercise it in an absolutely honest manner, with respect for the individual and his liberty. The fear of psychiatrists that many people experience is indeed the fear of a man they think capable of piercing their intimate secrets without their knowledge. The first time my wife and I had dinner with two of my psychiatrist friends, she confessed to me on leaving that she had felt quite ill at ease: she had the impression that their penetrating looks observed all the secret movements of her soul, that nothing escaped them. Since then she has formed a solid friendship with both of them.

Many people have also admitted to me that, if they were afraid of being operated on, it wasn't so much the fear of the operation itself as the fear of anesthesia and of revealing some personal secret in their

[3] "Médecine, quatrième pouvoir?" Introduction by Emmanuel Mounier, *Esprit* (March 1950).

sleep. To respect the individuality of our patients is to respect rigorously their secrets, life's secrets, to keep from asking prying questions, to respect their right to secrecy, even when they tell us they have something on their heart they don't have the courage to express. This is the price of the patient's confidence in his doctor, this confidence which is necessary to the practice of medicine. I truly believe that the reason so many people confide in me so much is because I am not curious. Curious people are avid for the revelation of secrets, and they get very few, for everyone protects himself against their prying, just as all wildlife flees when it realizes it's being pursued by the hunter. On the other hand, the more secrets you are told, the less curious you are. Every man, to feel respected as an individual, needs to feel absolutely free to say what he wishes and to keep as a secret what he wishes.

III TELLING SECRETS, OR THE SECOND STAGE IN THE FORMATION OF THE INDIVIDUAL

This thought takes us back to our little Frances. When her mother asked her if she had walked on the right or left side of the street, she answered capriciously to protect herself against this inquisition. But to a little friend, she is perhaps going to tell the truth: that she took the side of the street where there were no stores, just because this friend does not ask her questions, and also because she experiences pleasure in proving her friendship for her by this confidence. This contrast is naturally going to increase gradually, to bear on events more important than which sidewalk she took. More and more she will hide from her mother things that she will tell a chosen friend in order to make a closer friend of her.

So therefore, if keeping a secret was the first step in the formation of the individual, telling it to a freely chosen confidant is going to constitute then the second step in this formation of the individual. Freedom is what makes the individual. Keeping a secret is an early assertion of freedom; telling it to someone that one chooses is going to be a later assertion of freedom, of even greater value. He who cannot keep a secret is not free. But he who can never reveal it is not free either.

In reality, what we brought out at the beginning of this study, this need that the child begins to experience to not tell everything, to have a secret, a personal one, was a part of the process of becoming an individual rather than the blossoming of the personality. One can not become a person without first being an individual, without freeing himself from the clan, from parental domination, without becoming aware of his own individuality, which has a right to secrecy. But if one remains at this stage, one remains an individual, rather than a person. By opening out, by telling one's secrets—but freely this time—one becomes personally linked with those to whom he reveals them, and becomes fully a person thereby.

That is true even when the child opens his heart to his mother or father. It is easy to see that the criterion of the maturity of a person is his freedom. As long as the child remains controlled, as long as he does not dare hide anything from his parents, he remains in a childish dependence with respect to them. But when he has freed himself through secrecy, then he can form an intimate relationship as a person, even with his parents, and no longer just as a child, by telling them secrets that he is free to keep if he wishes to do so. Frances did not choose her mother, whereas she did choose the little friend whom she is going to tell what she does not tell her mother. Now, choice is precisely the prerogative of the individual. She could now even choose her mother as confidante and friend; that would be an act of affirmation as a person, because she would have chosen her freely.

I recently went to see my grandchildren in their new place in the country. After a little while, they took me by the hand and led me solemnly toward a dark thicket, where they had made a sort of hut. This is an example of this little secret world the child needs and which he animates with all his imagination. My grandchildren drew back the branch which represents the door; they let me go in; they took me into their secret and demonstrated their affection for me by this privilege.

However, to free himself from his parents, the child must necessarily form friendships outside of them. And parents are irritated because he does not always choose the friend they would have desired and because he tells this friend what he doesn't tell them. Their jealousy is aroused, not only because their child begins to hide something from them, but because he tells it to his friend. They especially feel when that happens that their child is getting away from them, that he is becoming a person. Their parental jealousy with regard to their child's friends can take on tragic dimensions, even if parents only express it in a veiled fashion, even if they are not at all aware of it, which is often the case. They work to run down the friend who has gained so much influence over their child: "I don't like for you to see that boy so often; he doesn't have a good influence on you; and besides, you mustn't be exclusive: it seems you can't get along without each other!" You see: parents preach freedom after having found fault with their child for seeking freedom from them. Moreover such parental reactions estrange even more the child who from now on turns to his friend for support. Indeed it must be noted that this is a fortunate development and that the misfortune of other children has been in having parents who were too excellent, too free of jealousy, who never gave them reason for a legitimate revolt against them.

Thus, a person's development is a result of a double action, alternative and complementary: an action of refusal, then an action of surrender. There is an experience in holding one's tongue, then an experience in speaking. Moreover, it is a question not only of words, but of gestures and attitudes. Thus, a woman, sitting down in my office, keeps on her very dark sunglasses, although I was careful to seat her with her back to the light, so she could see me better than I could see her. After a quarter of an hour of discussion, she takes off her glasses, muttering: "Will you allow me?" If I allow her! But I also know what that gesture means: "I am now a little less afraid of you; I don't have such a strong desire to hide." Moreover it is clear that this gesture gets all its significance from the very fact that until then this woman kept on her sunglasses. People who open their hearts too freely rarely bring us secrets of a liberating nature.

This double action of withdrawal and giving of self is going to be repeated throughout a person's life and on every occasion. In order to give one's self, it is first necessary to possess one's self; but it serves no useful purpose to possess one's self, if it is not in order to be able to give one's self. It's a subtle game, but full of shades of meaning, which at every moment indicates the degree of reciprocal relationship between the two speakers. If one speaks more intimately than the other, there is a certain uneasiness, for there is no longer equality; there are no longer two persons on even terms, but a lesser and a greater. Those who open their hearts too easily to everyone and who don't know how to keep any secrets are not taken seriously. Those who never give of themselves, but restrict themselves to impersonal ideas, repulse or bore others. Those who ask too many questions seem importune. Those who don't ask enough seem distant.

Naturally, everyone has his own private thermostat. There are some people warmer than others; there are some more talkative, who endlessly tell innumerable secrets already known by everyone; there are others, more taciturn. There are some whose voices are only imperceptible murmurs; there are some so noisy they disturb everyone, and, in a restaurant, tell their secrets so loud that no one misses them. The Dutch don't have any curtains on their windows even in the evening. They like for passers-by to see their sumptuous furniture, the inside of their home, their calm and model family life. The French surround their homes with high walls and close the blinds even during the day.

But what I had been describing is much more profound than these crude appearances. A Dutchman is no more ready to open his heart to someone than a Frenchman, a noisy person than a taciturn. A truly intimate word from a man who is usually reserved bowls us over. And also it is for him the occasion of a much richer experience than a flood of secret revelations spread carelessly by someone else. Even silence has its different tonalities according to the moment. It can be a haughty refusal, but it can be a real gift of self.

Our little Frances has grown up now; she has become an adult; she has blossomed out. She had to learn little by little this delicate and significant game, this game of secrecy and of openness, of silence and of speech; how far can you go in telling secrets to this person and that person, and where must you stop? It is quite an art, and like all arts, it is learned at the price of many trying experiences. It depends on this prudence that the philosophers of antiquity held as such a worthy virtue. There is also the right time to say each thing; there is what must be said immediately, the opportunity to grasp on the fly, and there is what must be put off, what must be ripened before expressing. There is also the time which must be allowed to others, the silences which must be respected in order not to offend. An animal has only reflexes; he can not put off his reaction for even the most earnest request. What is peculiar to man is his ability to choose, not only his response, but also the moment of responding.

There is therefore at every moment and in our relationships with every person, without our even being aware of it, a small measure of our personal secrets that we reveal and a small measure that we keep. By that may be measured the maturity of a person, his personal freedom. Children who do not know how to keep a secret, chatterboxes, men or women who don't know where to stop, or cannot, are powerless to establish with others a proper person-to-person relationship. They cannot resist the vain pleasure of telling all sorts of secrets that they are proud to know, and because of their lack of inner freedom fall under the subjection of others. But close beings, incapable of expressing anything truly personal, are condemned to the prison of their mental solitude. Every being has need of self-expression. Why do men like to meet in a cafe, women in a tearoom, young people at a bar? They meet to tell each other their little secrets. There are some people who must be taught to speak out more and others who must be taught to keep quiet; and each is as difficult as the other.

We shouldn't believe, however, that everything is a matter of convention in this universal social game, or determined by natural temperament. What counts is precisely a certain slight deviation from accepted conformity and a little beyond the natural behavior of a man. For example, take someone who suddenly speaks to you in an intimate tone that he had never used with you, who tells you what he had never dared tell anyone. Because he was ordinarily so reserved, you are rightly all the more touched. You sense there a mark of extraordinary confidence. Suddenly, he has become a friend. He has chosen you for a friend; he has chosen you for a confidant. At this very moment an infallible bond has been established between him and you, this bond which the philosophers call "interpersonal."

Moreover it is not only between him and you that something essential has taken place: it is also within him and within you. One becomes a person by means of this genuine and intimate encounter. No one discovers himself in solitude, by turning inward on himself and by analyzing himself. It is by giving one's self that one finds himself. To tell a secret is to give one's self; it is the most precious gift, the one which touches the most. This friend has become himself a person by this victory over himself, over his natural resistance to open his heart, over his timidity and his constraint. He experiences an extraordinary feeling of liberation. The dimensions of his being are suddenly increased; he has breached the wall within which he was suffocating. By becoming transparent for you, he has become transparent for himself.

He has also made of you a person at the same time, because he has chosen you as a confidant, because he has entrusted his secret to you. And this favor arouses in you an outburst of reciprocity, frees you, you too, of your restraints; you can, in your turn, in this atmosphere of unusual confidence, tell him some secret you would not have thought you would ever dare reveal. That is real friendship, this exchange of secrets through which each of the two partners feels that he is growing, becoming more profound and more mature. For most people that is one of the greatest and most beautiful experiences of adolescence, this age when they make the passionate discovery of the value of friendship, this real communion which is established by a mutual gift of secrets.

As for me, I was so uncommunicative that I didn't have this experience until long afterward. For in the presence of a close being, one closes up too, and opens up only in the presence of someone who is ready to open up, himself. Because of the tardiness, however, the experience had an even greater effect on me. The doors of my prison were opening; my life was completely transformed by it, to the extent that I became a privileged man to whom many other men bring their secrets.

However, this intuition, this flair that people have of guessing to whom they can open their hearts, requires indeed a certain maturity. Saint Francis de Sales said that one must choose his confessor out of ten thousand. Of course, he meant it to apply to sacramental confession. But it is no less true of this secular and mutual confession in which are forged deep friendships. Most of the unfortunate experiences in this respect, that have been related to me, went back to adolescence. In the highly emotional eagerness which characterizes it, a boy or a girl happens to confide a very precious secret to some friend who won't be able to keep it. That is a real catastrophe. The disclosure of a secret is a betrayal, a violation of the person. The very process which could have been so valuable for the formation of the individual is going to block the evolution of the person if he fails because of indiscreetness. Whoever has been betrayed once, in that way, when he had given himself in complete frankness and honesty, becomes distrustful for a long time, at times for his entire life.

To receive a secret constitutes then an enormous responsibility always. A confession which may constitute a remarkable liberation of a man, if he is sure the secret will be kept, will on the other hand be destructive if his secret is disclosed. I am not speaking here of shameful secrets alone, but just as much of precious and marvelous secrets of an exceptional mystical experience, for example, that quite often a man doesn't dare tell anyone for years. I have the most scrupulous conception of the secrecy that the revelation of another man's secrets prescribes. It often happens that someone is astonished that I have told my wife nothing of what he told me, when it's a question of rather commonplace things he would have discussed with her without any qualms. (Let him tell her himself!) He may then as a result question our relationship as a man and wife. But that consists of telling your own secrets, not those of others.

On the other hand, I relate at times in my books, with the permission of my wife, anecdotes of our life which concern her as much as me, or even more than me. She accepts it as her participation in our work. It is not a question of my literary work; it is a question of the human work to which we are both consecrated together: we both seek, in our relations with others, she with the people she meets, I with those who consult me and the readers for whom I write, to go beyond the conventional level of general and theoretical ideas, to speak in a more personal way. For we have learned that what helps men most in their search for the truths of life is to hear other seekers speak of their actual experiences. A person is not an abstract entity; it is our real personal life, such as we live it, and we have so much difficulty in expressing just as it is. However, my wife doesn't hide from me the fact that it pains her to see certain of our secrets delivered thus to the printer. It matters little to her that these lines be read by some distant Japanese or Australian, but it is a different matter for some nearby person, who knows us personally, a relative, or a friend.

It can be seen that all that is very subtle. What we fear in the disclosure of a secret is that it may reach the ears of some particular person. That's also why an inhabitant of Geneva prefers to consult a psychotherapist at Zürich, and a person at Zürich comes to Geneva. That is also why a faithful Catholic goes sometimes to confession in a distant parish where he is not known. Some disclosures of secrets may seem rather harmless to us when they are not at all for the person who disclosed them. There are not any big secrets and any little secrets. What gives our secrets their emotional value is the fact that they are ours and they affect us.

However, there are indeed some secrets especially burdensome, and there are many more in the world than you would believe. There are secrets which poison the atmosphere of a family for a lifetime. An illegitimate child the mother had before her marriage, that she hid out, and whom she goes to see mysteriously once a year. Or the fact that the youngest son is only a half-brother. When must he be told that the man he regards as his father is not? And how difficult it is! Even more difficult if the father himself does not know or pretends not to know because his wife has never dared confess it to him. Perhaps this child will never be told; he will always be deceived about his identity, which is a violation of his person.

Many couples don't have the courage either to tell a child soon

enough that they adopted him as a very small child. He will find out about it brutally through one of his schoolmates who will throw it in his face as an insult or through an unknown, unfeeling governmental clerk when he goes to get a passport. There are many other secrets kept with anxiety: an ancestor who formerly collaborated with the enemy; another who led a loose life; another who went bankrupt; a brother who turned out badly as a homosexual or a convict, that has been read out of the family life but whose reappearance is feared. And there are also secrets of the family's domestic life. This man honored and admired by all, who is a member of the parish council and of committees of many moral and social activities, has atrocious quarrels with his wife. Both of them and their children are afraid the noise will reach the ears of their neighbors. He can be cruel, beat his wife brutally; he doesn't understand himself and wonders with anguish what his colleagues on the committees would think if they knew about it.

And now, from the shame of others, we move on to the shame each of us has for his own secret conduct. There are not only the wrongs committed in a moment of aberration. There are also the wrongs that a person has never been able to free himself from, in spite of the most sincere resolutions, and which he continues to do. There is that bottle of port or whiskey hidden carefully in the bookcase he can't get along without. There are some pornographic drawings shut up in a drawer. There is a prostitute that a very respectable father of a family visits regularly in great secrecy. There is a portfolio at the bank that has never been declared for taxes. There are some very childish hobbies for which you could be ridiculed by those who know you only in your public life, where you are always, as Sartre says, "on the stage." There is that strange weakness that a man so decided, even authoritarian, in his public life, may have in his private life with respect to his wife who takes advantage of it. There are those stupid expenditures which another cannot resist and which he would not dare confess to his wife, to whom he is always preaching economy. There are a thousand little cowardly, despicable acts which we surprise ourselves by committing.

IV THE PSYCHOTHERAPEUTIC SITUATION

There is an imperceptible borderline between the revelation of a secret and confession, for both consist of the confession of secrets. And every secret is a weight whose confession unburdens the soul amazingly. How true it is that in our contemporary world, in certain countries at least, the psychotherapists have taken, for many people, the place of religious advisers. The churches are somewhat to blame. For centuries clergymen alone concerned themselves with souls. But they often did it in an off-handed fashion. Some clergymen think they have done their full duty by listening to a man for an hour or two. And if this man comes back too often, they say to themselves: "He's a sick man, making mountains out of molehills," and don't listen to him anymore except in an absent-minded fashion, without suspecting the importance of human problems which the experiences of sick people reveal. Then, all of a sudden, Freud had enough love for men's souls to listen to them with infinite patience for hundreds and thousands of hours!

Freud and his pupils have thus reaped for us an unbelievable harvest of new knowledge. A knowledge of sick people first, an understanding of those to whom they dedicated themselves. But also a truer and deeper knowledge of man in general. Our entire concept of man, our entire anthropology, has been overturned. Freud has taught us how much men need to unburden themselves in order to discover themselves. He has revealed the highly therapeutic virtue of this simple fact of speaking without restraint and without pretense. Now, well people have need of that remedy as well as the sick. He invented learned words to describe what takes place: catharsis, affective transference. But we can express these phenomena in a simpler language: to tell your secrets, to experience thus the human communion which we all need.

Yes, there you have the essence of psychotherapy, of every school. And all the dissident disciples of Freud, Jung, Maeder, Adler, Rank, have rendered due homage to the genius of their master who had opened the way to a medical movement, the psychoanalytic movement, which has finally been revealed as the source of a whole movement of very rich thought. The churches themselves, after having fought it, derive benefits from it now, to the extent that clergymen overcome their prejudice. The treatment of the religious soul, which had become archaic for so long in relation to the other disciplines of the ministry, has been thereby renewed and brought back into its rightful place.

We find again in the psychotherapeutic situation all the elements we have brought out. By unburdening himself to the doctor, by telling him his secrets, those he did not tell to his parents, the patient frees himself from the latter. Often, at the beginning, he hesitates. He has scruples about telling things which do not concern him alone, but also other people: his parents, his brothers and sisters, his teachers, his friends.

He is afraid of creating unjust judgments on them if he relates what he has resented and suffered. It's because he is still dominated by a childish principle: parents are taboo.

And moreover, throughout a series of psychotherapeutic consultations, we find this rhythm of alternation of withdrawal and surrender which we have already discussed. Everyone has a presentiment right away that the condition for the success of such an undertaking is a complete transparency, that it's a question of being true all the way, of telling all one's secrets. But no one succeeds first off. You can only come closer and closer. It is never a definitive state, but a movement, and a vacillating movement at that. There are resistances, withdrawals, blocks. And then new deeper unburdenings which denote as many liberations.

But above all, like the friend chosen by the child of whom we were speaking a short while ago, the doctor is a freely chosen confidant, a dependable confidant, who will not betray any secret, a confidant to whom you can reveal what you have never told anyone. However, he's a little different from a friend: even if the doctor and the patient are of the same age, the doctor's function makes him an elder. He plays the role of a father, or at least of a big brother. His patient is going to form bonds with him by the confession of his secrets, and even with the Freudian technique in which the doctor observes a scrupulous silence.

It is well known what a rigorous reserve Freud recommended to the doctor in the course of the classical psychoanalytic treatment. Not only does the doctor not answer any of the questions the patient often asks with anguish, but even more, he conceals himself: he is behind his patient who is stretched out on a divan and who cannot read his facial reactions. Therefore there are no mutual reactions between them, in the sense I described it, for example, between two friends who mutually reveal secrets to each other. There are cases in which this Freudian technique is absolutely necessary.

However, even in this situation, there is more mutual reaction than was first thought. After having studied the affective transference, that is to say, the feelings that the patient experiences about his doctor in the course of the treatment, Freudians have been obliged to examine the countertransfer, that is to say, the feelings which are aroused in the heart of the doctor himself. No matter how reserved and quiet he tries to be, he participates actively in the event. Something takes place then between the doctor and the patient, and it is something mutual, since both of them take part through each other.

Moreover we are going to see this reciprocity increase more and more in the course of the development of psychotherapy. In the place of the hidden silent doctor, Jung and Maeder are going to place the doctor face to face with his patient. We have gone beyond the Freudian monologue. There is a hint of dialogue. Maeder will be the first to speak of personal contact, a term which has the sound of a deeper interaction. But the doctor still remains very discreet; he scarcely intervenes except for questions. Finally, today, Frankl advocates out and out dialogue: the doctor must keep the dialogue going; he must accompany the patient in all his questions which preoccupy him and must not avoid any of them. He must only observe a strict ethical neutrality and be sure not to let his own personal convictions enter into play.

The medical treatment of the individual is not a psychotherapeutic technique. It characterizes an attitude of any doctor, a surgeon for example, in his relations with his patient, man to man, or person to person. When it is practiced by a psychotherapist, it leads him, as

Maeder,[1] and later Plattner,[2] have demonstrated, to free himself, at the opportune time, from last reservations still noted by Frankl, and to accept a relationship of complete reciprocity. The doctor can then involve in the dialogue his own person, his own spiritual life, his judgments of personal values, his experiences that he had had, and his own secrets. It has been feared that such a complete reciprocity might lead to damaging proselyting and preaching. But all depends on the spirit which animates the doctor, on his true respect for the individuality of the patient. My experience is that, on the contrary, this attitude achieves the greatest interpersonal bond between the doctor and the patient while bringing the latter to the greatest ethical and spiritual autonomy at the same time. It seems to me that there are remarkably fewer difficulties due to transference in this open reciprocity than in the concealed reciprocity of classical psychoanalysis.

However it is necessary to have just the right amount. I have already emphasized it in the situation of friend to friend. Balint,[3] after Maeder,[4] pointed out that in such an endeavor the therapeutic agent is the doctor as a person. He also pointed out that this treatment by a person plays its role not only in psychotherapy but in all of medicine, for all patients, whether those of internists, surgeons, or practitioners, have secrets which weigh on their hearts. All need to express them, and it is not possible for them to do so, as long as the doctor does not give

---

[1] Dr. A. Maeder, *Vers la guérison de l'âme* (Neuchâtel: Delachaux & Niestlé, 1946).
[2] Dr. P. Plattner, *Médecine de la Personne* (R. K. Arsenblad, April 1950).
[3] Dr. Michael Balint, *Le médecin, son malade et la maladie* (Paris: P.U.F., 1960).
[4] Dr. Alphonse Maeder, *La Personne du médecin, un agent psychothérapeutique* (Neuchâtel: Delachaux & Niestlé, 1953).

them the time or the receptive atmosphere, as long as he questions and examines them in a purely objective manner. All need a personal relationship with their doctor in which they can unburden themselves freely. And this unburdening can at the same time contribute to their cure and to a better comprehension of their case by the doctor.

But Balint also points out that in medical schools we are not taught to what extent we ought to use this medicine of our own person. We find then again this problem of the proper amount we have spoken about: how much must be said and how much must be kept silent; how far to go with gestures, attitudes, and silences. Every doctor exercises, according to Balint, an "apostolic function," that is to say, an ethical and spiritual influence over all his patients. He communicates to them, consciously or not, intentionally or without realizing it, his concepts of life, his philosophy, his beliefs. Basically, he always gives up, more or less, his secrets, to the extent that he gives of himself to his patient. Reciprocity is not so much a question of words: it is expressed even more so in an attitude, an emotion, a look, a silence.

The examination of this psychotherapeutic situation leads us to a finer and deeper analysis of the problem of secrecy: in the psychotherapist's office there is more than the presence of a patient who tells his secrets and a doctor who listens to them with attention and respect. There are two men in search of their own secret, of this more secret secret of which they do not have conscious knowledge, which escapes them, but of which each has a presentiment in the decisive role that it plays in his life, which is somehow the elusive secret of his existence.

Man has always been incomprehensible to himself, but he is more tragically conscious of it today than in the last century. The discoveries of psychoanalysis have revealed to him that there is in the depth of his

soul a secret closet whose key he has lost. What is there in this closet of the unconscious? What feelings, what desires, what emotions, what memories, what impulses, what hopes, what remorse? He can only perceive a few colorless traces, a few troubling and uncertain reflections. There is a mysterious inner secret down there which is frightening. The more progress a man makes in self-analysis, the more he realizes what is still missing and will always be missing in the discovery of himself.

I believe that it is one of the principal causes of the anguish which characterizes man of today and which the existentialists have also made us feel. He indeed knows that he is always more or less on stage, that he strives to seem what he wants to seem in order to hide better what he is, but he does not know what he is hiding or what it is. He indeed knows that no matter how beautiful his life may be, it is only a fresco that he has painted on the door of his secret closet. That is exactly what Jesus Christ was describing, long ago, when he spoke of "whited sepulchres" (Matt. 23:27, K.J.V.). But what is there then in this sepulchre where all the repressed rubbish of all humanity as well as of our own past is rotting?

A powerful psychological censorship mounts guard over those secrets. Man senses that even if he succeeded in breaking it open, the secret of secrets, the final secret of his personal existence, would remain incommunicable, inexpressible, even to himself. There are some fleeting moments, precisely during the psychotherapeutic dialogue, when doctor and patient perceive to some extent that bottomless abyss of their souls. They cannot represent it by words, at most by tears, silences, or images.

Images are the language of dreams. Our dreams are the veiled form through which our subconscious self whispers to our conscious self secrets which are ours but which we did not know. That is responsible for the particular emotion that we always feel on telling a dream. We indeed feel that we are revealing thereby to someone else an important and secret part of ourselves whose clouded meaning still escapes us, even if we have a slight presentiment of it. We are also upset when someone tells us a dream. Every dream is a revelation of a secret, richer and more mysterious than any secret formulated in words.

V THE MARITAL SITUATION

In a like manner, man and wife can also have an incomparable experience of communion by telling each other their dreams. We are going to find once again, in the marital situation, all the elements we have studied about secrecy. First of all, note that modesty is only a matter of this withdrawal, this aloofness, this secret, of which we have spoken, and which must necessarily precede the gift of self to confer on it all its value. Even parents must delicately respect the modesty of their children, as it develops in their souls, for, if they do not, they seriously wound them and compromise thus their sexual life of the future, as I have learned from innumerable interviews. Young men or girls who lack modesty, who surrender their bodies too easily, will not know either, in its fullness, the enjoyment of the gift of self in their sexual lives. Modesty is the normal instinct which every person upholds in order to reserve himself so that he may give himself more completely to the partner chosen for his entire life.

Chosen! Yes, all that we have said about the choice of a special friend, of a confidant, is going to take on now a new importance and a new dimension. For, in life, it is possible to have many friends, even many very close friends, at the same time or successively, while everyone senses intuitively that the love relationship forms a bond so complete that it cannot be divided. The sexual bond is the gift of the supreme secret, supreme intimacy, of the finest, most personal secret, one's own body. The fiancé, or the fiancée, is the unique partner, chosen definitively.

There is inscribed in the human soul a law of all or nothing in love. The gift of one's body is only the sign of this decision to make a complete gift of self which will imply also the mutual gift of all one's secrets. "We will be happy," proclaim the engaged couple, "for we have decided to tell each other everything always." They will perceive later that it is not so easy as they thought. But they begin. There is, moreover, a necessary parallelism, a necessary synchronization between familiarities of the body and revelations of secrets of the mind. The body and the soul are the two rails of the individual: for the train to go without grinding, the wheels must move forward together on the two rails. It is as unfortunate to bypass all the stages of physical effusions without opening one's heart to each other as it is to speak to each other more and more intimately without exchanging either a kiss or an embrace. What a wonderful engagement when these two ways of getting to know each other and of giving of self move forward harmoniously together!

It is the miracle of love which volatilizes these barriers of secrecy and reserve which held each of the couple shut up within himself. When you love and feel yourself loved you can express yourself. You discover yourself by expressing yourself, at the same time that you discover the other partner. There are indeed sometimes confessions quite difficult to make, but what seemed impossible becomes possible. This engaged couple relate their lives to each other, as a patient relates his to a psychotherapist. Here, however, there is a complete reciprocity. That is what makes love a spiritual reality, for everything that is spiritual is reciprocal. There is an uneasiness when one of the couple surrenders easily, while the other, which was my case, obstructed in his emotional availability, cannot express himself except in general, abstract, and impersonal considerations. And every little detail is of importance, not only the notable events but the tiny little secrets that one dares tell because he senses that everything interests the other who is eager to know all, hear all, understand all. That is what confers on this mutual discovery during the engagement a character of revelation.

However, as in the psychotherapist's office, it is when it's believed that all has been said that the real discovery begins. It will be necessary to come to grips with the conscience, to rediscover some memories whose importance had escaped them. Throughout married life, this progressive and parallel knowledge of the partner and of self must continue. And that will be accomplished only by stages, by successive jerks, by an alternation of withdrawals and difficult surrenders. The honeymoon passes. Each of the couple perceives that he had created some delusions for himself. Each had projected his total ideal into his partner. In the zeal of their early love, they had seen each other just as they wished rather than as they were. They had endowed each other with qualities they didn't have; they did not see in each other the defects which were however quite manifest, quite displeasing, and quite tenacious.

Each begins to make judgments on the other that he is tempted to keep secret in order not to wound. There are also some subjects which irritate the partner and about which it is better not to talk in order not to disturb good marital relations. A wife hesitates to speak to her husband of certain reminiscences for fear they will support the judgments that he makes, or may make, on her and her parents with whom there are now some disagreements. Now, each of the couple, in the desire for peace and without realizing it, begins to break often the promise they had made to tell each other everything always.

They withdraw within themselves and speak only of commonplace impersonal things. They begin to become strangers to each other. Such actions of withdrawal happen in all homes and, like Frances and her mother, they become aggravated if the other asks too many prying questions: "What's the matter with you? Why are you becoming so secretive? You don't tell me anything anymore. Don't you love me anymore? I feel you're hiding something from me."—"Of course not, I assure you; you're making it up; I'm not hiding anything from you." But the uneasiness can develop to the point of creating a storm, which will be quite distressing, to be sure, but worthwhile however. Successful marriages are not those in which there has never been conflict, but those in which conflict has served a useful purpose. For in anger one may say suddenly and brutally in an exaggerated fashion truths he should have said long ago.

Or the couple may start really talking to each other again quite simply when coming home from a movie or a lecture, or when having dinner together in a restaurant. The dikes are broken this time, not by an explosion, but by an imperceptible crack. The discussion is prolonged far into the night. They have a strange feeling that everything is beginning all over again, that they have regained this true mutual unfolding that they had lost. They explain their conduct. Each has secrets to divulge and secret reservations to confess. Hope is reborn that the marriage will not be just a flash in the pan but a marvelous adventure of life together, endlessly renewed. This man and wife are beginning to understand each other. They discover how many secrets, many important ones, they had begun to hide from each other, the misunderstandings, the prejudices that their criticisms of each other involved. As soon as someone truly opens his heart, certain misunderstood aspects of his personality, the obscure motives of his behavior, become clear; our opinion of him must be revised.

One woman told me that when she got married, her mother had given her some advice: "Don't tell your husband everything; to maintain her prestige and keep her husband's love, a woman must retain a certain mystery for him." What a mistake! It fails to recognize the meaning of marriage and the meaning of love. Transparency is the law of marriage and the couple must strive for it untiringly at the cost of confessions which are always new and sometimes very hard. They must strive unceasingly to re-establish this transparency, for it constantly becomes tarnished, without their knowing exactly why.

As a matter of fact, there will always remain enough mystery about the other for both of them! The knowledge of someone else, as moreover the knowledge of self, is never a completed state but a periodic movement which is refound and pushed further ahead precisely because it had been lost. The best way to misunderstand your wife or your husband is to suppose you do know him, for when you think you know him, you don't seek to understand him any longer. It is always through the exchange of secrets that man and wife re-establish their unity and develop. For the secret becomes fossilized. Moreover they must always overcome the fear of not being understood, a universal and extremely paralyzing fear of being judged. It is also often a fear of being laughed at by the other who might misunderstand the value of an experience or a feeling, or the gravity of some scruples.

This progress toward transparency is no small matter for it must continually be renewed and it must unceasingly overcome new obstacles, but it is indeed worth the trouble, not only in order to build your happiness together and to create a wholesome family atmosphere for the children, but also in order to develop yourself, instead of staying in a rut, to enrich each other, to learn something new about each other unceasingly. Marriages may be observed, for example, in which the husband is incapable of expressing his love except by carnal desire, whereas the wife, passionately fond of sentimental communion, accepts sexual love with some reticence. The conditions on which both a living marriage and a living personality are based is to explain your conduct, never to capitulate, never to make up your mind about any misunderstanding, for life itself is only a struggle to begin anew without ceasing against everything which threatens death, a victory never achieved but a succession of costly victories.

It takes time. Few husbands and wives know how to reserve it for each other. Rather they allow themselves to be swept along in the hustle and bustle of existence. They believe they are unified because they do a lot together; they go to the theater or church together, or they go fishing or play bridge together. They will perceive some day, tragically, that they have run side by side without ever having truly found each other. To be "no longer two but one" is not only a question of participating in the same events and having sexual relations; it means to let our partner look deeply into our soul, to not have any secrets from the other.

It means to have no private garden in your life, protected by a barrier and a stop sign for one-way traffic going the other direction, except for professional secrets and secrets of others which must be scrupulously kept. It means, for example, to have no secret about money matters from each other, which is rather rare and very important. For the money that one spends is always an indication of the value he puts on everything. To consider together and to decide together about every expenditure is always conducive to a spirit of unity. That requires facing up to the very concept each has of life as well as the matter of tastes.

There are many husbands who are careful not to tell their wives how much they earn—and wives too, today, who often have the idea that their own income is personal money and that it is not any business of their husband's what they do with it. A husband fears, if he tells his wife the total of his salary, that it might incite her to spend more while he's preaching economy unceasingly. But there is no wife more spendthrift than the one whose husband practices this secret policy. For she doesn't share with him the responsibility of the conduct of their affairs. Kept in the dark, she cannot acquire the necessary judgment that man and wife continue to improve by a constant open discussion.

Then, this wife whom her husband reproaches continuously for spending too much, and whom he tells he will be ruined if she keeps it up, perceives that when it is necessary, or when he really wants to, her husband can suddenly spend sizeable amounts. Therefore he must have secret reserves at his disposal. Quite often, each hides from the other a part of his expenditures, for fear of encouraging the other to spend more, the husband how much he spends on hunting trips, or the wife how much she spends at the beauty parlor. But she really does it for him, she thinks quite sincerely. She goes to the beauty parlor so often as a tribute to him, without exactly realizing, perhaps, that she goes there also because she can tell secrets to her hairdresser. There are some hairdressers who are real psychotherapists. There are others who broadcast all the secrets of the town.

And then, you have a husband who relates his day's activities to his wife. He went to the dentist, and he had an important conference with his department heads. He has really been busy! But he doesn't tell that in between he found the time to go chat in a cafe with an old friend his wife doesn't appreciate. Because the friend is divorced and leads a dissolute life, because he's a good talker, she claims that he has a bad influence over her husband who is always aggressive toward her when he has seen him. And there are many other secrets: for example, correspondence that the husband carefully hides in his desk. At times, on the contrary, a husband ostensibly lets a compromising letter stick out of his pocket, because he can't bear the secret any longer, but doesn't have the courage to confess it openly.

It's always difficult to keep the promise made to tell each other everything, whether it is a question of use of time, or money, of a rigorous marital fidelity, or less grave things but no less important: an emotional reaction, an apparently stupid fear, a rather petty complaint, ridiculous scruples, a naïve whim, a hope which will probably never be attained, a perhaps unfair suspicion, a little white lie, a strange and disturbing religious experience, a dreadful premonition—doubtless without foundation—an idle complacent fancy, or an agonizing worry. Moreover, even between man and wife this right proportion and right time we have talked about is necessary. When a husband asks me if he ought to tell his wife a particular secret, it is impossible for me to know if she is at the right stage to hear it.

We see, therefore, that it is difficult and delicate to tell everything. Always one of the couple must help the other to open up. Now, nothing helps a husband in that matter like extreme prudence on the part of his wife and vice versa. Each needs to feel respected, free, not spied on. Curiosity and lack of tact stand in the way of telling each other secrets. If the other is talking, it is important not to interrupt with enthusiastic approval, untimely comments, or premature advice. I have seen husbands become mute as the result of such an assault. Quickly, they pulled up the drawbridge and remained from then on shut up in their fortress.

Then too, husband and wife have many secrets in common they must keep zealously. The husband who tells his mother everything his wife does, or the wife who recklessly tells the secrets of her married life to a friend, demolishes their happiness in a devastating fashion. And when this takes place, they have even less restraint in divulging their private difficulties. To respect scrupulously your partner is to respect your marriage and yourself. I would never take the liberty of reading a letter addressed to my wife left open on the table or even a postcard unless she asked me to do so.

Moreover I am very happy that she is as discreet and doesn't set foot in my workshop where I like to be alone to putter, and also that she doesn't comment on its terrible confusion which serves me as an antidote for the excessive constraint of ordinary life. Likewise here at the hotel where we are spending a vacation. To write this book, I have settled down in a sitting room off to the side. My wife is careful not to join me there. She knows that her presence, even without speaking, would disturb me in my work, whereas strangers could play bridge next to me without disturbing me.

But how many wives understand such matters? How often is it that they drive away their husbands and lose their close relationship by their insistence? Couples who become identified to the point of not being able to leave each other's side and of never having a difference of opinion are less unified than they believe. For the very reason that they are not free, and you must be free to become united. Their so perfect togetherness is often only a conscious overcompensation for a claim for autonomy which has been repressed into the subconscious.

See how subtle it is: if I forbid my wife to take a hand in my affairs by some authoritative statement, I am upsetting our good relationship. But if she subtly refrains from all that could seem obtrusive to me, she enriches, on the contrary, our harmony by delicate nuances. Most men are more sensitive than they will admit and than their wives think. Unfortunately, the wives devoid of this tact are the ones to whom husbands are obliged to tell to stay out of what doesn't concern them, so that the wives who are the most eager for the revelation of secrets are the ones who get the least. Also the most intimate couples continue to become more so whereas those who have shut themselves off from each other will dig even deeper the ditch which separates them. . . . Unless . . . unless something takes place which re-establishes the dried-up stream: in either of them a change of attitude, or a sort of inner conversion.

In a little while, after finishing this page, I am going to meet my wife, and we shall go take a walk together under the brilliant sun and the deep shadows of Malaga, or climb the winding paths of its fortress in the splendor of the sunset. We won't talk much; we are both rather silent by nature. Our life is so interesting that we have lost our taste for chit-chat. However, we are interested in everything, a pretty dress that goes by, a child with a mischievous smile, a kitten sleeping in a listless unconcerned fashion, what cafe has the best coffee. But a single word is enough to create a closeness.

We are silent by nature, especially I, so far as to be concerned that it will offend others. For example, during the war I wondered what my comrades were thinking. What officers can find to say to each other in their mess is unbelievable. There are naturally favorite themes which are taken up again every day, for example, an argument over the relative merits of wine from Vaud and Valais. In such matters I feel quite incompetent and don't know what to say. Yet I liked all my army companions very much. So, once I took advantage of the situation when my captain and I were waiting for a train at the Interlachen station to ask him about it. I hesitated for a long time, then suddenly I took the bull by the horns: "You must consider me very taciturn; does that bother you?" After a pause, he answered: "No, not at all; there are some silences of absence, but yours is one of presence." I was reassured!

Moreover, for husband and wife there is a royal road to mutual discovery without constraint: to commune together before God and to exchange the thoughts received in this meditation. In that case, the requirement of total frankness does not come from the partner and his questions. It is required of us by our own loyalty to God and to ourselves. Inevitably, in this silence, memories, impressions, remorses, convictions, surge forth that we would have preferred to keep secret, even to avoid considering and certainly not formulating clearly. But the nature of meditation is favorable for this because of the mutual respect imposed by the presence of God. And when you have jotted down your thoughts on paper in your notebook, it is easier to speak about them frankly. It is for that reason that I have seen many couples give up meditation that they had practiced for a while, because they were no longer prepared to play the game strictly, to tell each other no matter what idea received in this communion with God. Before God there is no secret, and couples who make a practice of meditation together are assured of knowing the most intimate thoughts and feelings of each other.

VI GOD'S SECRETS, OR THE THIRD STAGE IN THE FORMATION OF THE INDIVIDUAL

Yes, before God, there is no secrecy, and this truth has considerable significance. The most powerful means of getting to know ourselves is to allow ourselves to be examined by God and to listen to what he has to say to us, for he knows us better than we know ourselves. He knows all our secrets. Nothing escapes him. Jesus said he counted all the hairs of our head (Matt. 10:30). The psalmist cries out (Ps. 139:1, 7, 8, 11, 12):

O LORD, thou hast searched me and known me! . . .
Whither shall I go from thy Spirit?
Or whither shall I flee from thy presence?
If I ascend to heaven, thou art there!
If I make my bed in Sheol, thou art there! . . .
If I say, "Let only darkness cover me,
and the light about me be night,"
even the darkness is not dark to thee,
the night is bright as the day;
for darkness is as light with thee.

That is what upsets many people! "What provokes me," writes a very
devout woman to me, "is that he always has the last word!"

God knows all our secrets, and yet he wants us to tell them to him.
He knows all our needs, all our desires, all our fears, and all our hopes,
and yet he wants us to express them in prayer. That is a paradoxical
fact which for a long time was difficult for me to understand. Why pray
then, since God knows all? When we talk to someone we tell him what
he does not know. But everything we say to God, he knows already.

> Even before a word is on my tongue,
> lo, O LORD, thou knowest it altogether,

says the psalmist (Ps. 139:4). If we bring our secrets to God, therefore, it isn't to make them known to him. Why, then?

Well, it is because God respects our person, because he waits for us
to tell him our secrets ourselves, freely, as little Frances told her little
friend, as the patient told his doctor, as the husband his wife. He is
waiting for us to make this demonstration of our love and confidence.
God's waiting, infinitely patient and discreet, is very stirring. He is
waiting for us to choose him as confidant, even though he already knows
everything about us. What matters is not that he learn it but that we
tell it to him and that we manifest thus our will to let us be known to
him. It is also because a confession does not give a complete release
unless we make it to God, before whom we feel ourselves responsible:

> When I declared not my sin, my body wasted away
> through my groaning all day long. . . .
> I acknowledged my sin to thee,
> and I did not hide my iniquity;

I said, "I will confess my transgressions to the Lord";
then thou didst forgive the guilt of my sin. (Ps. 32:3, 5.)

One may say, it seems to me, that God respects our secrets. He accepts the fact that we refuse to speak, for many years; he waits; he does not force us. And we find here again this first action which characterizes the individual, this withdrawal, this right to secrecy, which must precede the confession of a secret for it to have the value of a free act. Yes, in our relations with God, we find again this alternation of refusal and surrender which denotes the formation of a person. God wants us to become persons. That is why he respects our revolts, our reticences, our disobediences which alone confer a genuineness on our returns, our confessions, our adoration. He who has never doubted has never found true faith either. He who has never said "no" to God cannot genuinely say "yes" to him.

Moreover we find again in our relations with God also the reciprocity which characterizes everything spiritual. God is waiting for us to choose him as confidant, because he, first, chose man as confidant. God, first, told his secrets to man. God spoke to him, God speaks to him every day; he demonstrates thereby that he considers him a person, a conversational partner, free to listen or to stop up his ears, to answer or to refuse to answer.

God speaks, God approaches man and speaks to him familiarly.

That is an astounding fact. It is the essence of the biblical message, that of the Old Testament; also that of the New Testament, when God comes himself in Jesus Christ and reveals himself in Jesus Christ; he accepts also that misunderstandings, conflicts, and withdrawals alternate with rich meetings, experiences of intense communion; when

God respects the right of man to reject him as far as the Crucifixion; when Jesus himself on the cross feels himself abandoned by the Father; when the darkness of Good Friday and the secret of the tomb precede the glory of Easter and give it all its brilliancy.

Moreover this fact fills even the early pages of the Bible, then all those of the history of the chosen people, then all those of the prophets: God speaks to man, he reveals himself to him! Revelation is the communication of God's secrets by God himself. We would never know anything for sure about him, his mercy, his intention, his work, his plan, if he had not said it himself. What distinguishes him from the impassive God of philosophers is that he did not remain all alone, that he chose for himself a partner "in his image," with whom he can enter into conversation. And it is always he who speaks first; everything begins with the Word of God, that of man is never anything but a response.

Moreover it is not only to mankind in general or to the great prophets that he speaks. He speaks to each of us; he is personally interested in every one of us; he speaks personally to each of us and he listens to each of us personally, and that is what completes the process of making a person of us. The person, in the full sense of the word, is man in personal relationship, not only with others, but with God.

Hence, the third stage in the formation of a person. Man remains more or less a child, unconscious, irresponsible, an automaton activated by his instincts and reflexes, so long as he has not had the personal encounter with God, so long as he has not accepted the difficult dialogue with God. The first stage in the formation of a person was a withdrawal, becoming an individual by the creation of a personal secret. The second stage was the free communication of this secret to someone else freely chosen, and out of it the experience of love and the interpersonal relationship with another. And the third stage is to have this double experience in our relations with God, to feel ourselves distinct from him, to choose him also freely, to tell him our secret and to know thereby the interpersonal relationship with him, the experience of the love of God. That is likewise the significance of the parable of the prodigal son, with his long absence and his regained unity with his father, so marvelous that his elder brother who had never left home is jealous of it (Luke 15:11-32).

However, to enter into dialogue with God is no small affair, no more so than the psychotherapeutic adventure or the marital adventure. There is an evident parallelism between the three, but the last two are only a sort of limited prefiguration of the only truly decisive experience, the encounter, not of a doctor nor of a partner in marriage, but of God himself. Moreover the three situations offer analogies. We always find these alternations of withdrawal and surrender, of refusal then gift of self, of secrets and then confessions.

I have seen many believers who found it hard to accept these inter-mittences of the spiritual life and the fact that terrible reversals, times of darkness and forsaken loneliness, in other words secrecy, can follow tremendous success. They were able to accept this in their relations with men, because the latter are not perfect, which always makes it possible to think it's their fault if we have difficulty in getting along with them. But with God, perfection itself, how can we explain these difficulties?

Well, God is a God who speaks, but he is also a God who keeps silent; he is a God who reveals himself to us, but he is also a God who hides from us. Saint Paul declares it in front of the Areopagus at Athens: God "is not far from each one of us" and yet he determined "that they should seek God, in the hope that they might feel after him and find him" (Acts 17:27). Feel after him! That expresses very well this mixture of light and darkness, of revelation and silence, of certainty and uncertainty, which always denotes our progress toward God. God is not a dead God, who would allow himself to be dissected at leisure: he is the Living God, with all life's palpitations and rhythms.

And it is precisely because of this difficulty that our intimacy with God develops unceasingly. The success of psychotherapeutic treatment or of the unity of a married couple is not always achieved once and for all. It is renewed and deepened through many storms. If we could easily snatch from God all his secrets, they would no longer be so precious. The knowledge of God is not a completed state, but a perpetual and difficult discovery. God has a plan for us, for each of us at every moment. What is this plan? That is his secret. We strive laboriously to decipher it. We feel after him. Quite often the light bursts forth from our mistakes. We dimly perceive sometimes some design of God, we hear his call, and then we begin to doubt again, plunged into perplexity.

And all this seeking requires much secrecy. "But when you pray," says Jesus, "go into your room and shut the door and pray to your Father who is in secret..." (Matt. 6:6). Meditation is the secret and patient waiting for God's secrets which he may whisper to us in the secret of our heart. All religions have had the sacred sense of the secrets of God, the esoteric. Great mystics, those who penetrate most deeply into the secrets of God, speak of them prudently, reservedly, difficultly. The greatest secrets are inexpressible. At times, in the encounter with God, we have the impression of discovering life's secret, but we also sense that it is incommunicable. It is a secret between God and us which must be respected reverently.

Immediately after the most wonderful experiences, we sense all that is still lacking in our knowledge of God. This final mystery of every being, that we have never been able to penetrate with any man, which always escaped us, is found again on quite another scale in our approach to God, with the immeasurable distance which always remains between the creature and his Creator. We shall never perceive anything but a few flashes, a few reflections of him. That was the experience of Moses who had fought and lived so close to God. When Moses asked him to let him see his glory, Jehovah answered him: "Behold, there is a place by me where you shall stand upon the rock; and while my glory passes by I will put you in a cleft of the rock, and I will cover you with my hand until I have passed by"; (The secret!) "then I will take away my hand, and you shall see my back; but my face shall not be seen" (Exod. 33:21-23).

"For now," writes Saint Paul, "we see in a mirror dimly, but then face to face." Yes, then, he says, "when the perfect comes" (1 Cor. 13:12, 10), after trial by death, at the time of the coming of the Master. Then, there will no longer be any secret.